FETISHES

and Carvings of the Southwest

by
OSCAR T. BRANSON

Design, Color Coordination and Photography Arrangements
by
ETHEL BRANSON

**Photography
by
NAURICE KOONCE
Tucson, Arizona
and
PETER BLOOMER
Flagstaff, Arizona**

**Treasure Chest Publications, Inc.
P.O. Box 2659
Santa Fe, New Mexico**

**Mailing Address:
P.O. Box 5250
Tucson, Arizona 85703**

Printed in Phoenix, Arizona by Associated Lithographers

LEEKYA DEYUSE

This is a portrait of Leekya Deyuse the famous and very prolific Zuni indian carver. It was painted from photographs belonging to his family and friends by Rod Goebel, a Taos artist.

Leekya was born about 1889 and lived in the pueblo of Zuni where he was much loved and greatly respected. During his 77 years, he developed his own unmistakable style and produced numerous carvings that are collected and cherished by a great number of people. At auctions his art commands the highest prices.

Leekyas' carvings are easily recognizable and have a unique quality that everyone likes and appreciates.

Leekyas' name has been mispelled in published articles, magazines, and catalogues. This is the correct spelling and pronunciation; Deyuse (DAY-USE-SAY).

3

Prehistoric white stone figure, possibly of a bobcat because of its spots and upturned tail.

Brown travertine figure of a mountain lion with its tail up over its back found in a cliff dwelling.

Ancient turquoise figure, possibly of a wolf. Showing marks of abrasion with prehistoric stone tools.

Brown banded travertine figure of a coyote with a stone arrow point bound by sinew. Found in a cave.

White alabaster stone horse, stained yellow by corn pollen. Probably early Navajo.

Black jet horse figure found with the one above in a Navajo medicine bag. These two show considerable wear from use.

Painted sandstone figure probably of a bear with a shell arrow point bound by sinew.

INTRODUCTION

The Southwestern Indians have made and used fetishes since very early times. The usual concept of a fetish is an object in the form of a living thing made of any material, usually attractive, but sometimes quite unattractive. In archeological sites dating well over 1000 years, fetishes are being found that equal or surpass some of the best carvings being done today.

All the tribes make and use them, especially the Zunis who have developed them to the greatest extent. The Zunis have become the most skillful carvers and produce the most appealing figures on the market today. The Zunis have been the suppliers of personal charms and amulets to other Southwestern tribes for many generations. It is no surprise when the present demand and popularity of the fetish necklace stimulated the Zuni carvers to produce quantities of attractive carvings.

We have tried to show by the photography in this book that the present time is not the only period in history when the fetish necklace was popular. Imagine the desire of other Indian women around the year 1100 when they saw their sisters wearing the fetishes shown on page 7.

The Navajos, of course, make their own fetishes and carvings. They also will barter from the Zunis figures of horses, cattle, sheep or goats in the belief that these amulets will help keep their flock free from disease and insure propagation.

Among the Zunis, there is a fetish for almost any unknown phenomenon, including those for use in hunting, war, initiations into cults or societies, propagation, diagnosing and curing diseases, gambling, and even the detection and protection against witchcraft. In the indian society, a fetish may belong to an individual, a secret society, a clan or it may be the property of the entire tribe. A fetish is thought to bring good luck and, if treated properly and with veneration, will help or give power to its possessor. The most prevalent belief is that the power is supposed to reside in the spirit dwelling within the fetish rather than the fetish itself.

Fetishes, amulets and talismans are related objects and people seem to have different meanings for each, but the feeling and belief behind all of them is related. Not only the indians, but people all over the world since the beginning of time, have made and used fetishes. The belief in them and the use of them is still very much alive. Many of the world's most intelligent and successful people carry a favorite talisman with them at all times and are genuinely frightened if it is misplaced or lost.

These figures represent a chronology of fetish carving from prehistoric to the present time.

Navajo horse figure of white calcite with banded travertine "prayer stick" bound to it by rawhide.

Contemporary carving of a bear. Out of treated or stabilized turquoise. Not really a fetish.

A malachite horse carved by Neil Natewa of Zuni.

Turquoise carving of a fox by David Tsikewa dating from the 1960's.

Brown banded travertine bear carved by Leekya in the nineteen-forties.

Abalone shell horse carved by Leekya, probably one of his early pieces of the middle nineteen-thirties.

Figure of a fox with large turquoise eyes carved from the lip of a helmet shell.

THE FIRST FETISHES— CONCRETION FETISHES

The earliest of fetishes are called "Ahlashiwe" or stone ancients by the Zuni indians. They are naturally formed stones that seem to resemble people or animals, sometimes made more realistic with the features accentuated by a carver. They are considered very powerful and were formerly thought to be ancient animals or people turned to stone.

An old and very realistic hematite concretion fetish with a face carved on it. There is another small concretion resembling a bird tied upon it, together with bits of turquoise and a tiny abalone shell. These adornments are usually votive offerings given to the fetish in appreciation of services rendered or sometimes to give the fetish more potency.

Sections from fossil shells called ammonities, when this fossil is found broken apart the pieces resemble small animals and are held in great esteem by the indians.

A very old medicine bag containing two naturally formed stones—white for female, black for male—formerly used in phallic rites.

Courtesy Don and Nita Hoel, Sedona, Arizona

PREHISTORIC FETISHES

A thousand year old tiny turquoise pendant one-half inch high.

Cliff dwelling sculpture by Gregory La Chapelle
Courtesy Fenn Galleries, Santa Fe, New Mexico

A group of fetishes from prehistoric times found in and around ruins and cliff dwellings. The materials are some of the same that are used today; turquoise, travertine, shell, very fine grained sandstone, basalt and pottery.

PREHISTORIC FETISH NECKLACES

This necklace was put together from pieces sifted out of the debris at a ruin on private land on the east fork of the Gila River in southern New Mexico.

The tiny fetish carvings in the circle were taken from this necklace, photographed natural size, and then restrung. They are made of banded serpentine. The tiny bird in the center is moonstone. They were made about a thousand years ago.

The interesting thing about these tiny fetishes is they resemble some of the finest modern carvings today except the cone shaped holes are much larger, having been done with a stone drill.

Prehistoric red stone mountain lion pierced for a necklace, natural size.

A prehistoric fetish necklace of black argillite with jet, red argillite and turquoise fetishes.

A prehistoric turquoise necklace with shell, travertine and turquoise birds.

PREHISTORIC STONE FETISHES

These are probably bear figures made by the ancient method of pecking a hard stone with a sharp stone and then smoothing by abrading with fine sand.

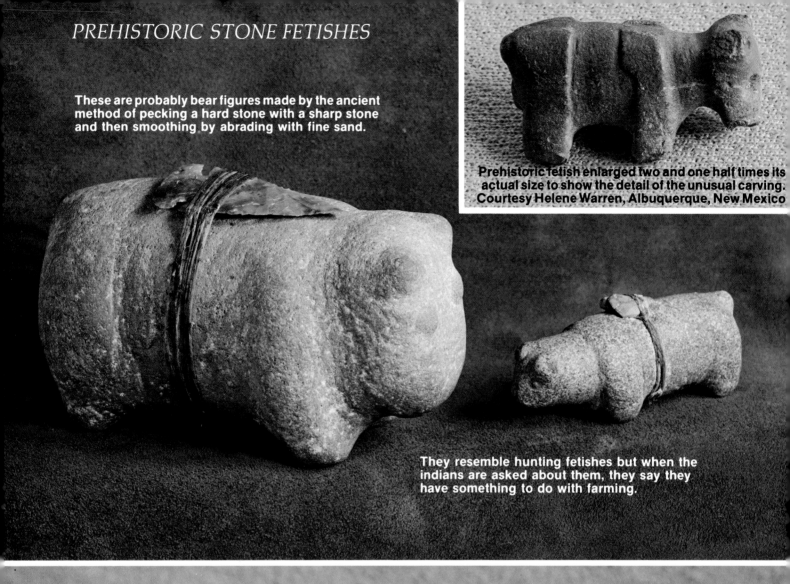

Prehistoric fetish enlarged two and one half times its actual size to show the detail of the unusual carving. Courtesy Helene Warren, Albuquerque, New Mexico

They resemble hunting fetishes but when the indians are asked about them, they say they have something to do with farming.

PAINTED STONE FETISH

Apparently a badger, showing traces of several layers of paint under the existing top layer. It is very old, most likely prehistoric.

Painted fetishes of this type are still used in Zuni. (See the page on fetishes of the six directions.)

Courtesy The Amerind Foundation, Dragoon, Arizona

HOHOKAM

These carvings of soft volcanic stone are evidently not fetishes but were possibly ceremonial containers of about the year nine hundred.

A light green serpentine fetish pendant found in a cotton field near Casa Grande National Monument was undoubtedly the prized possession of a Hohokam maiden over a thousand years ago.

Courtesy Helene Warren,
Albuquerque, New Mexico

Courtesy The Amerind Foundation, Dragoon, Arizona

TAOS POTTERY FIGURES

This group of ceremonial pottery figures is made of painted clay. Feathers and buckskin ears have been inserted into the holes made for that purpose.

A pottery pipe or cloud blower used in ceremonies to blow smoke rings.

These figures resemble many that are found in ruins.

Courtesy Don and Nita Hoel, Sedona, Arizona

PUEBLO BONITO

A painting of the ruins of Pueblo Bonito in Chaco Canyon, New Mexico by Rod Gobel, Taos artist.

Replicas of two fetishes found by George Pepper at Pueblo Bonito in the early nineteen hundreds.

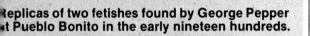

The turquoise inlay jet frog is three and one/fourth inches long and the turquoise inlay hemitite bird is two and one/fourth inches long.

A group of serpentine fetishes excavated from the ancient Pueblo of Casas Grandes in the state of Chihuahua, Mexico. There is evidence of this material having been mined in New Mexico, almost two hundred miles north. These carvings were made by the old method of pecking out a figure with a sharp hard stone and then abrading and polishing it.

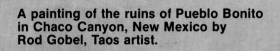

AN EARLY FETISH NECKLACE

This interesting necklace dates from around the early 1800's.

A fetish necklace of the 1920's or earlier composed of several kinds of shell, jet, and turquoise. It is strung on white clam shell beads or heshe.

It is made entirely from a brown banded travertine. Both the figures and beads were drilled by a sharp metallic object.

Private Collection

Courtesy Don and Nita Hoel, Sedona, Arizona

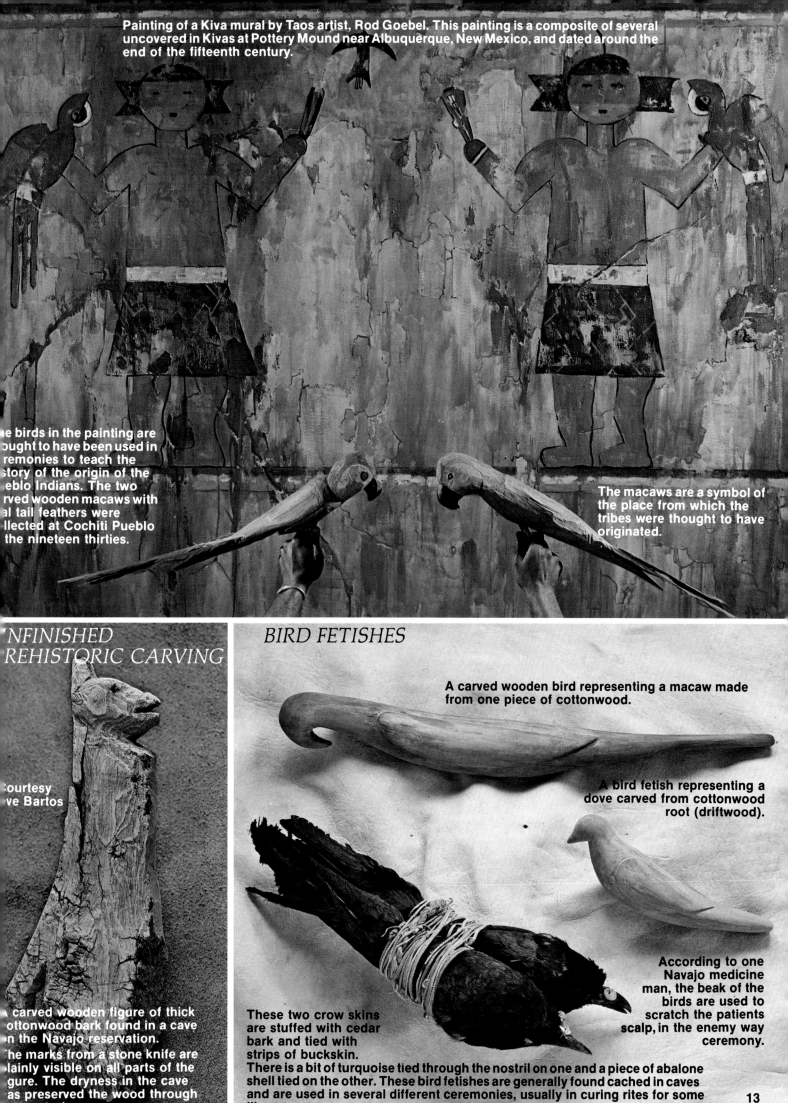

Painting of a Kiva mural by Taos artist, Rod Goebel. This painting is a composite of several uncovered in Kivas at Pottery Mound near Albuquerque, New Mexico, and dated around the end of the fifteenth century.

...e birds in the painting are ...ought to have been used in ...remonies to teach the ...story of the origin of the ...eblo Indians. The two ...rved wooden macaws with ...al tail feathers were ...llected at Cochiti Pueblo ...the nineteen thirties.

The macaws are a symbol of the place from which the tribes were thought to have originated.

...NFINISHED ...REHISTORIC CARVING

...ourtesy ...ve Bartos

...carved wooden figure of thick ...ottonwood bark found in a cave ...n the Navajo reservation. ...he marks from a stone knife are ...lainly visible on all parts of the ...gure. The dryness in the cave ...as preserved the wood through ...e centuries.

BIRD FETISHES

A carved wooden bird representing a macaw made from one piece of cottonwood.

A bird fetish representing a dove carved from cottonwood root (driftwood).

According to one Navajo medicine man, the beak of the birds are used to scratch the patients scalp, in the enemy way ceremony.

These two crow skins are stuffed with cedar bark and tied with strips of buckskin.
There is a bit of turquoise tied through the nostril on one and a piece of abalone shell tied on the other. These bird fetishes are generally found cached in caves and are used in several different ceremonies, usually in curing rites for some illnesses.

ETCHED PREHISTORIC SHELL

This lovely shell is neither a fetish nor a carving but the design has been etched with some type of natural acid. Made in the eleven or twelve-hundreds. Most assuredly it was a precious ceremonial object. It is from the Lewis Pueblo near Red Rock, Santa Cruz Valley, Arizona.

Courtesy Arizona State Museum, Tucson

Carving of a jet bear with turquoise eyes and red coral heart line by Neil Natewa. Made about 1955.

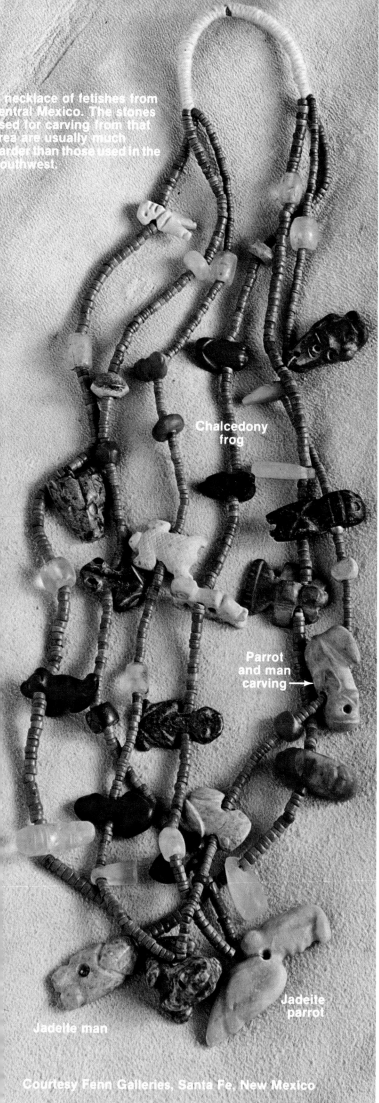

A necklace of fetishes from central Mexico. The stones used for carving from that area are usually much harder than those used in the Southwest.

Chalcedony frog

Parrot and man carving →

Jadeite man

Jadeite parrot

Courtesy Fenn Galleries, Santa Fe, New Mexico

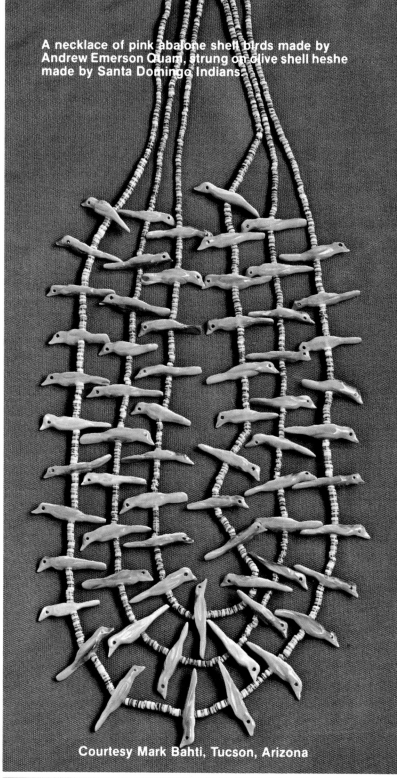

A necklace of pink abalone shell birds made by Andrew Emerson Quam, strung on olive shell heshe made by Santa Domingo Indians.

Courtesy Mark Bahti, Tucson, Arizona

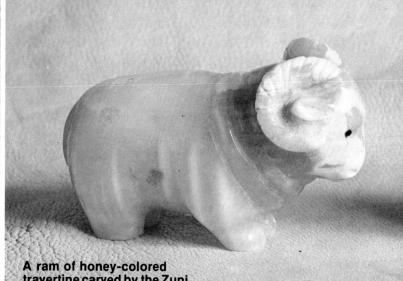

A ram of honey-colored travertine carved by the Zuni carver, David Tsikewa.

15

A Zuni necklace made during the nineteen forties of shell, jet and turquoise. The large spotted bird is of pink mussel shell. The spotted frog of conch shell.

Courtesy Don and Nita Hoel, Sedona, Arizona

Courtesy Fenn Galleries, Santa Fe, New Mexico

Glycymeris shell carved into a frog.

These shells traveled the trade routes from the gulf of California about the year nine hundred and were carved in what is now Arizona. The frog is strung on beads made from the olive shell which is still used by the Pueblo Indians of New Mexico to make beads.

Turquoise carving of a woman. Zuni carver Teddie Weahkee.

16

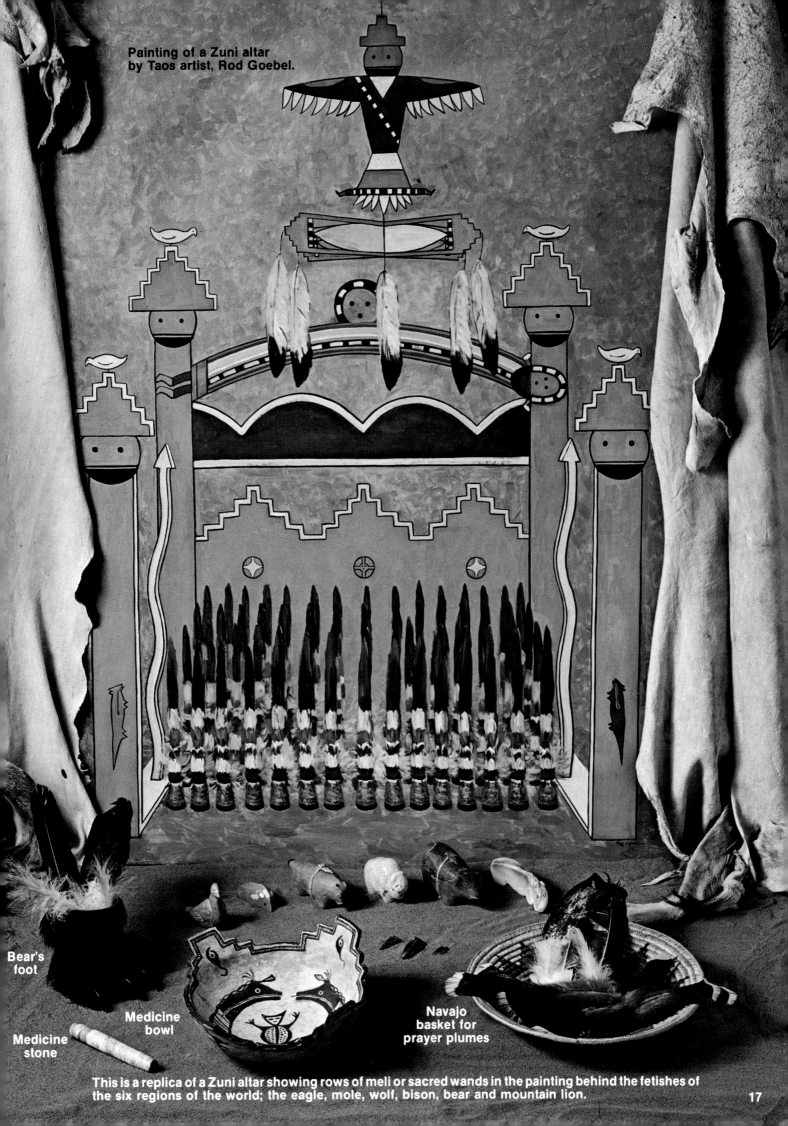

Painting of a Zuni altar by Taos artist, Rod Goebel.

Bear's foot

Medicine bowl

Medicine stone

Navajo basket for prayer plumes

This is a replica of a Zuni altar showing rows of meli or sacred wands in the painting behind the fetishes of the six regions of the world; the eagle, mole, wolf, bison, bear and mountain lion.

CEREMONIAL FETISH JARS

There are many types of fetish jars each with an accompanying set of fetishes. Some of them are:
Hunting fetish jar—the most numerous type.
Shalako jars, and there are many different ones.
Initiation jar—there are many societies and each has one or more jars.
The red ant medicine jar—several witchcraft punishment jars—
Weather and snake bite jar
War medicine jar
Gambling fetish jar
Fire making jar
Betting fetish jar
Scalp jar used as a repository for scalps with a turquoise left hand tied on one side and a turquoise left foot tied on the other.

On hunting society jars, the black material on the jar is usually the blood of animals of prey. It is said that it was human blood on the original turquoise jars.

Initiation jar hunting society.

Many of the rites connected with these jars are dying out because there are too few young men being taken into societies to continue their practices. When the last person dies that knows the prayers and ceremonies, the jar is usually buried or sold.

Courtesy Don and Nita Hoel, Sedona, Arizona

Mrs. Ruth Kirk wrote a series of papers titled "Introduction to Zuni Fetishism" while living at Zuni in the 1920's and 1930's. They were published by the school of American Research, Santa Fe, New Mexico in 1943. She describes a number of these jars, their use and beliefs and some of the ceremonies connected with them.

CEREMONIAL FETISH JARS

Ceremonial jars are the homes or receptacles for fetishes when not in use. The top is for putting the fetishes in or taking them out, sometimes buckskin bags of medicine are also stored there. The holes in the sides are for ceremonially feeding the occupants. The jars are usually kept on a shelf in the kiva or ceremonial room, about shoulder height and only a tiny pinch of sacred cornmeal or pollen tossed thru the hole, more as a token to show attention or respect rather than a lot of food. This is to appease the spirit of the fetish, to keep it happy.

An interesting paper about these jars titled "Turquoise Incrusted Pottery of Zuni" was written by Aileen Nusbaum and published in "The Masterkey" Volume 12 No. 3 May 1938 P.P. 79–99, Los Angeles.

Courtesy Don and Nita Hoel
Sedona, Arizona

ZUNI FETISH JAR

This ceremonial pottery jar and the sea animals accompanying it are probably part of an initiation set used to induct young men into the hunting societies.

The hole in the side of the pot is for ceremonially feeding the fetishes inside.

Water serpents
or
sea animals

Courtesy The Amerind Foundation, Dragoon, Arizona

ZUNI CEREMONIAL FETISH POT

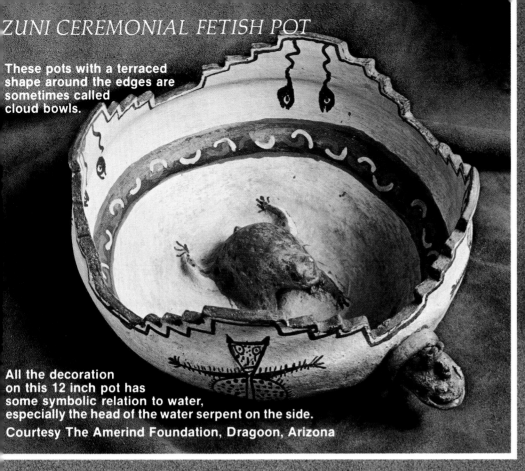

These pots with a terraced shape around the edges are sometimes called cloud bowls.

All the decoration on this 12 inch pot has some symbolic relation to water, especially the head of the water serpent on the side.
Courtesy The Amerind Foundation, Dragoon, Arizona

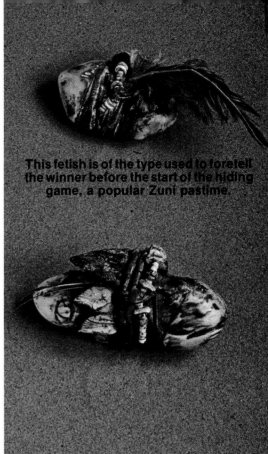

This fetish is of the type used to foretell the winner before the start of the hiding game, a popular Zuni pastime.

Deer antler fetishes probably from medicine jars used in curing rites.

This dual type fetish, representing the two sides, could have been used for luck in wagering in the stick race, formerly a popular Zuni game.

Fetishes of deer antler are used in numerous rites at Zuni, not merely because the material is readily available and easily carved but because it represents a link with a living animal and the spirit that dwells therein.

Courtesy The Amerind Foundation, Dragoon, Arizona

HUNTING FETISHES

These fetishes are displayed on a ceremonially tanned deerskin with the hair left only on the ears, tail and legs. These skins are an important part of the ceremonial costume and are worn as kilts by the Kachinas in many of the dances.

Eagle

Brown Bear

Coyote

Badger

Bag for the fetish on the hunt.

Tail

Mountain Lion

Wolf

Ears

A black basalt sighting stone with a groove to sight along at the prey when stalking it.

Two alabaster figures made and used by the northern pueblo Indians. There are many of this type made, but the taboos for selling them are so strict very few are available to collectors.

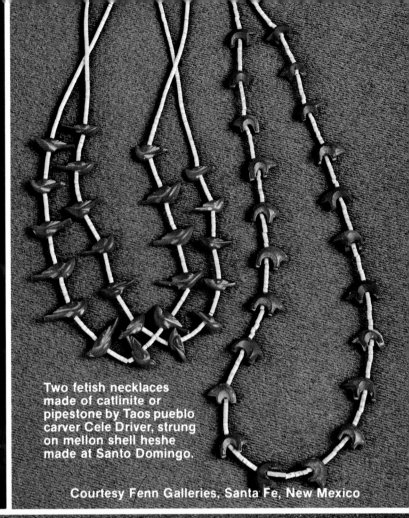

Two fetish necklaces made of catlinite or pipestone by Taos pueblo carver Cele Driver, strung on mellon shell heshe made at Santo Domingo.

Courtesy Fenn Galleries, Santa Fe, New Mexico

TURQUOISE LEFT HAND AND LEFT FOOT

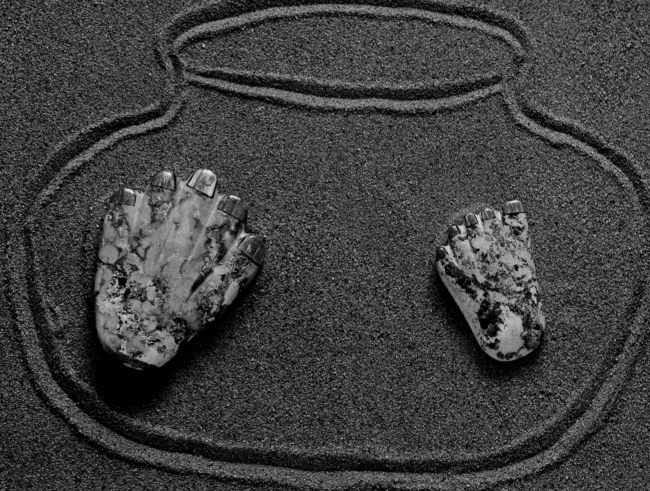

These carvings with the nails of red spondylus shell are like those seen tied on each side of the old scalp jars at Zuni. See page 18.

ZUNI DEER ANTLER FIGURES

These figures carved by artist Teddie Weahkee display a great talent. They are very rough carvings but seem so alive.

HOPI FETISHES

Two ancient Hopi fetishes shown in front of a pair of pahos or dance wands depicting a figure of the germ god. Beneath his feet are symbolic ears of corn.

POTTERY FETISHES

Pottery or baked clay figures were evidently quite numerous but when left exposed to the elements decomposed very rapidly. Also, it is difficult to determine whether these attractive animals were ceremonial objects or toys.

A pottery horse found in an old hogan on the Navajo Reservation.

This figure was found buried several feet under the corner of an old house when making a new road.

Acoma sheep figures evidently used in propagation rites.

A contemporary Hopi pottery figure.

During his lifetime, Teddie Weahkee carved a great number of things for many people, including those which were used in numerous ceremonies.

24

Courtesy Don and Nita Hoel, Sedona, Arizona

Glycymeris
shell hawk
carved by
Neil Natewa
Zuni

Eagle of the Zenith

Mountian lion of the north

Brown bear of the west

Gray wolf of the east

The six cardinal directions are each
represented by a mountain of a
different color. The fetishes of the six
directions are animals of prey, they are
animals of the hunt. Therefore they are
used as hunting fetishes. For example,
a hunter in quest of a deer would use a
mountain lion fetish because the deer
is the natural prey of the mountain lion.
Zuni fetishism can be extremely
complicated, for example, of the six
animals—each can have six varieties or
colors represented either by the color
of the material of which the fetish is
made or by painting or inlaying.

There are some exceptions, as these fetishes
are also used by medicine societies in certain
curing rites and various other ceremonies.

Badger of the south

Mole of the Nadar
Master of the Lower Regions

Courtesy Mr. Paul Huldermann
House of the Six Directions, Scottsdale, Arizona

ZUNI WAR GODS

Painting by artist Rod Gobel of Taos, New Mexico, taken from twenty-third Annual Report, Bureau of American Ethnology.

These wood carvings are considered one of the most powerful fetish type figures made by the Zuni Indians, carved only by certain priests and only from certain trees. For example, for the scalp ceremony they must be made from a Ponderosa Pine that has been struck by lightning. These figures play a very important part in the weather and rain-making ceremonies.

A lovely three-strand necklace with a tag indicating Lavina Tsikewa carved the birds. The beads were made by Santo Domingo Indians.

A dainty necklace of birds made of various colors of mother of pearl shell carved by Alice Quam of Zuni, New Mexico. The beads are probably pen shell of Santo Domingo Indian manufacture. Courtesy Jake Atkinson, The Apache Village, Tucson, Arizona

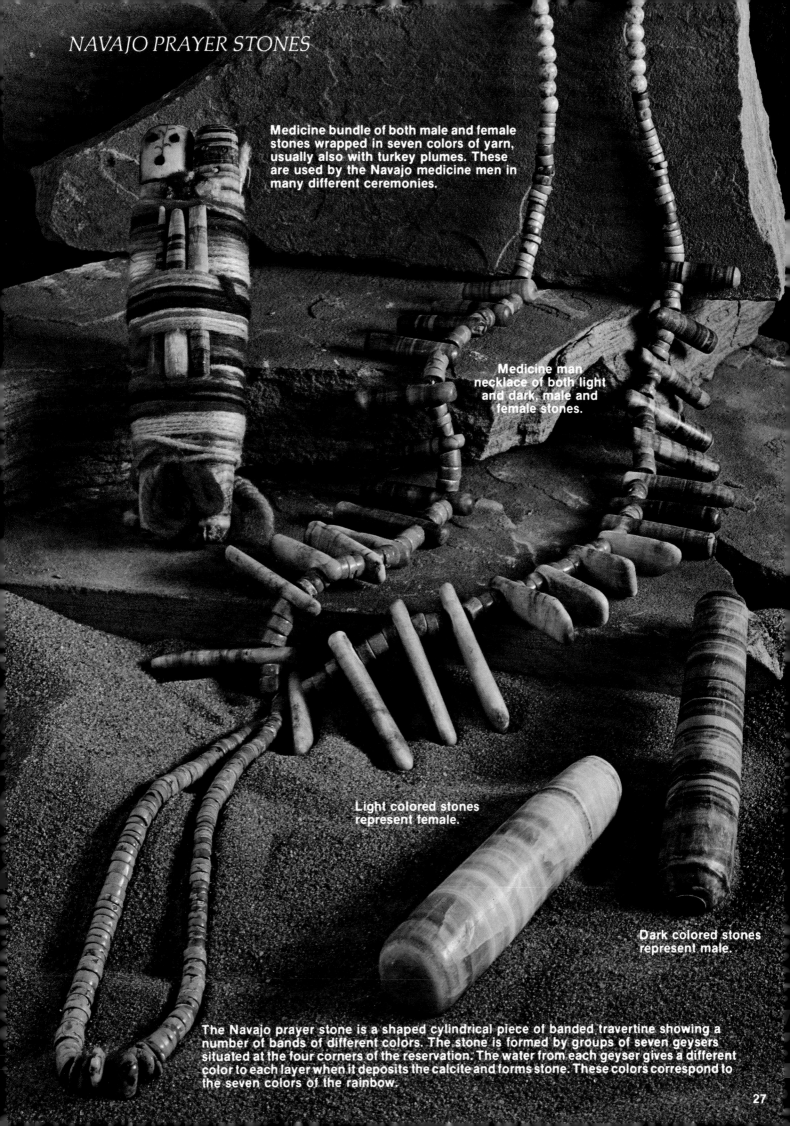

NAVAJO PRAYER STONES

Medicine bundle of both male and female stones wrapped in seven colors of yarn, usually also with turkey plumes. These are used by the Navajo medicine men in many different ceremonies.

Medicine man necklace of both light and dark, male and female stones.

Light colored stones represent female.

Dark colored stones represent male.

The Navajo prayer stone is a shaped cylindrical piece of banded travertine showing a number of bands of different colors. The stone is formed by groups of seven geysers situated at the four corners of the reservation. The water from each geyser gives a different color to each layer when it deposits the calcite and forms stone. These colors correspond to the seven colors of the rainbow.

Figures carved of deer antler produced solely for the tourist or curio trade. The sale of this type of carving supplements the Zuni income. These are not considered fetishes.

These doll-like figures are made of deer antler and resemble Kachina figures. They are sometimes called "altar dolls." Little is known about their use and occasionally one is attached to a ceremonial pottery jar.

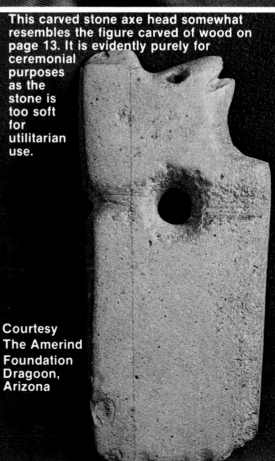

This carved stone axe head somewhat resembles the figure carved of wood on page 13. It is evidently purely for ceremonial purposes as the stone is too soft for utilitarian use.

Courtesy
The Amerind
Foundation
Dragoon,
Arizona

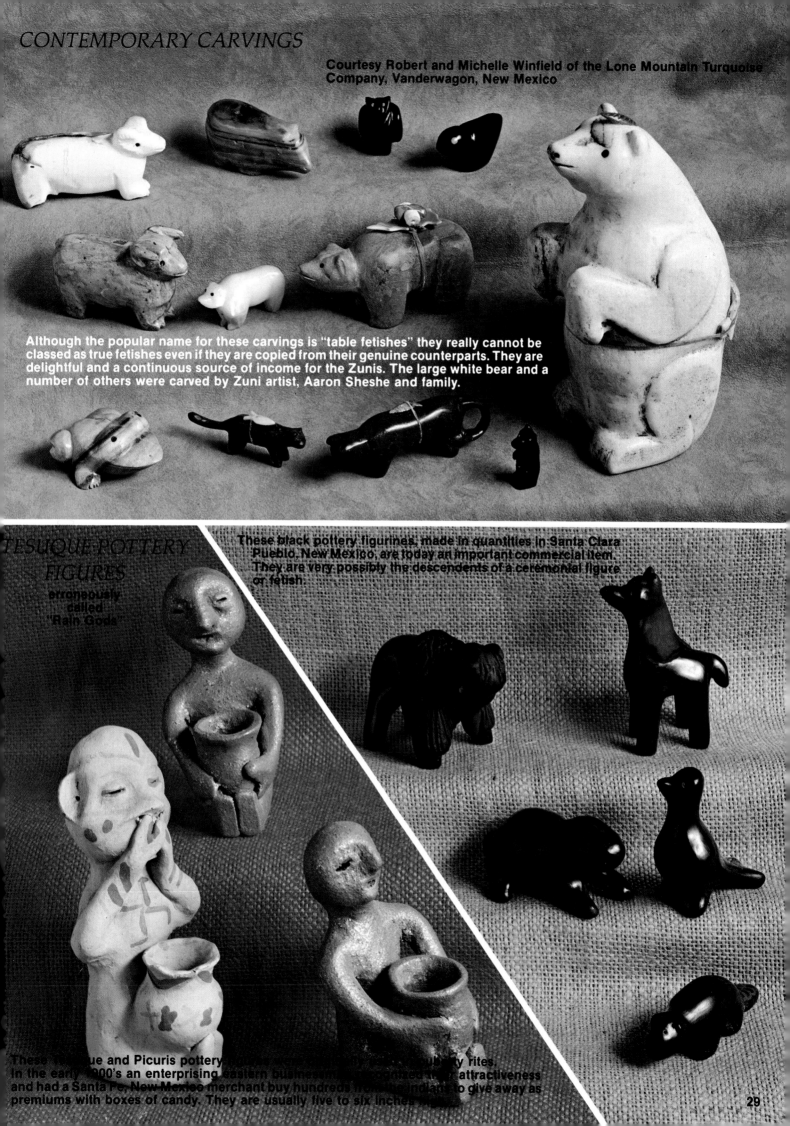

CONTEMPORARY CARVINGS

Courtesy Robert and Michelle Winfield of the Lone Mountain Turquoise Company, Vanderwagon, New Mexico

Although the popular name for these carvings is "table fetishes" they really cannot be classed as true fetishes even if they are copied from their genuine counterparts. They are delightful and a continuous source of income for the Zunis. The large white bear and a number of others were carved by Zuni artist, Aaron Sheshe and family.

TESUQUE POTTERY FIGURES

erroneously called 'Rain Gods'

These black pottery figurines, made in quantities in Santa Clara Pueblo, New Mexico, are today an important commercial item. They are very possibly the descendents of a ceremonial figure or fetish.

These Tesuque and Picuris pottery figures were modeled after ceremony rites. In the early 1900's an enterprising eastern businessman recognized their attractiveness and had a Santa Fe, New Mexico merchant buy hundreds from the Indians to give away as premiums with boxes of candy. They are usually five to six inches high.

29

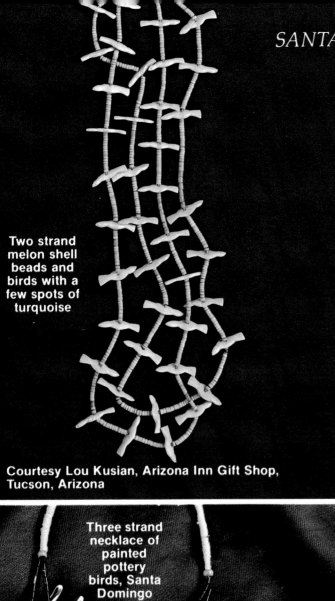

Two strand melon shell beads and birds with a few spots of turquoise

Courtesy Lou Kusian, Arizona Inn Gift Shop, Tucson, Arizona

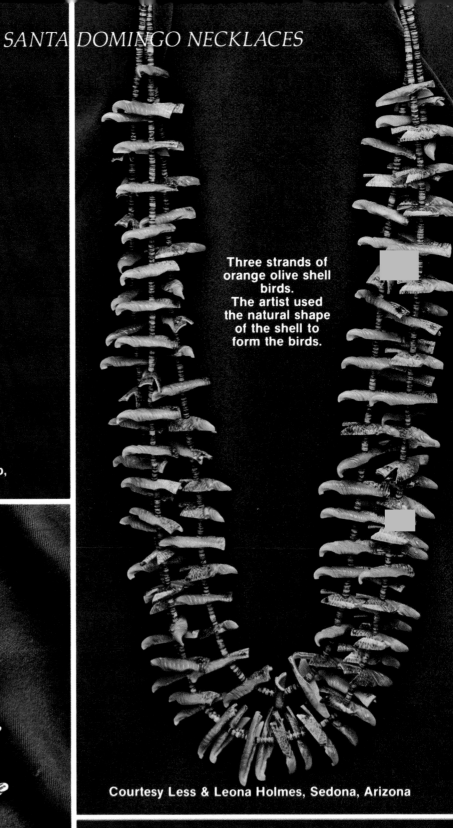

Three strands of orange olive shell birds. The artist used the natural shape of the shell to form the birds.

Courtesy Less & Leona Holmes, Sedona, Arizona

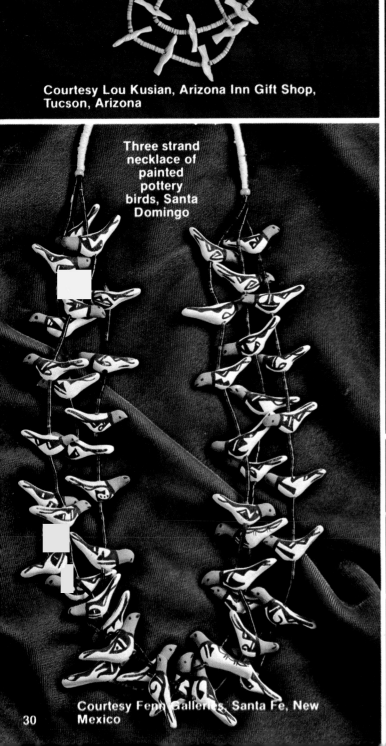

Three strand necklace of painted pottery birds, Santa Domingo

Courtesy Fenn Galleries, Santa Fe, New Mexico

30

The Santa Domingo Indians' anmistic beliefs have certain taboos about carving figures of birds and especially animals. Therefore the artists of these lovely necklaces wish to be anonymous.

It is sometimes popular at Zuni to mount carvings of turtles and frogs in necklaces instead of piercing and stringing with shell beads. The ingenuity of the Zuni artist and craftsman is infinite.

Courtesy Don and Nita Hoel
Sedona, Arizona

CARVINGS BY LEEKYA DEYUSE

Pronounced (DAY-USE'-SAY)

Travertine bear

Travertine
sheep

Bear head of
travertine
set in silver

Abalone shell bird

Travertine wolf

Serpentine frog

The pieces of turquoise, coral or arrow heads tied on the backs of the carvings are offerings or gifts to the spirit existing within the fetish.

Conch shell coyote

Pearl shell horse

Serpentine coyote

Abalone shell bird

Abalone shell horse

A variety of carvings by Leekya Deyuse showing the versatility of this great carver.

Serpentine bear

Conch shell bird

These four carvings are made of a massive mottled yellow and brown travertine rock found near Zuni, New Mexico.

Sheep

Turquoise wild cat

Abalone shell birds

Spotted Cowry bird

BISON OR BUFFALO

Carved from a piece of the giant purple lip oyster

This piece of turquoise was evidently almost this shape when found, very little carving was necessary.

Purple lip oyster

Bison carved from a piece of gold lip pearl shell

Neil Natewa carved this turquoise bison from a stone from Mineral Park, Arizona.

Turquoise

Carved from a piece of very fine grained sandstone

Blue gem turquoise

Carved of treated or stabilized turquoise

Carved from serpentine

Purple lip oyster from the Gulf of California

Evidently a stream pebble was found in this shape and a little carving formed it into a big horn sheep.

Turquoise

Carved from a piece of massive lepidolite from northern New Mexico

A necklace of light blue natural Lone Mountain turquoise birds made by Zuni Indian carver, Dorson Zuni

Courtesy Robert and Michelle Winfield
Lone Mountain Turquoise Company
Vanderwagen, New Mexico

COYOTE, WOLVES AND FOXES

Two moles

Mountain lion

The wolf, the coyote, and the fox;
it is often quite difficult to tell the difference between carvings of these animals.

35

A medicine bundle of male and female prayer stones. Used in many Navajo ceremonies. See page 27.

The whizzer or bullroarer is a flat wooden stick shaped to produce a buzzing sound when whirled at the end of a piece of buckskin thong or rope. Because of the buzzing or roaring sound, it was thought to possess a spiritual power. These two are very old, coated with black pitch and have turquoise eyes and mouth.

A Navajo medicine bag worn by the Navajo medicine men to carry fetishes and some medicine. These are usually lavishly decorate with silver button

The banded travertine bird is used in other ceremonies.

These are ancient medicine bottles made o rawhide and used to carry powdered medicine. The are considered to have special curing powers depending on their age and the medicine man to whom they belonged. Ver old ones are sometimes found hidden in caves.

Two medicine pouches both of which contain two horse fetishes and are used in many curing and fertality rites.

Courtesy Fenn Galleries, Santa Fe, New Mexico

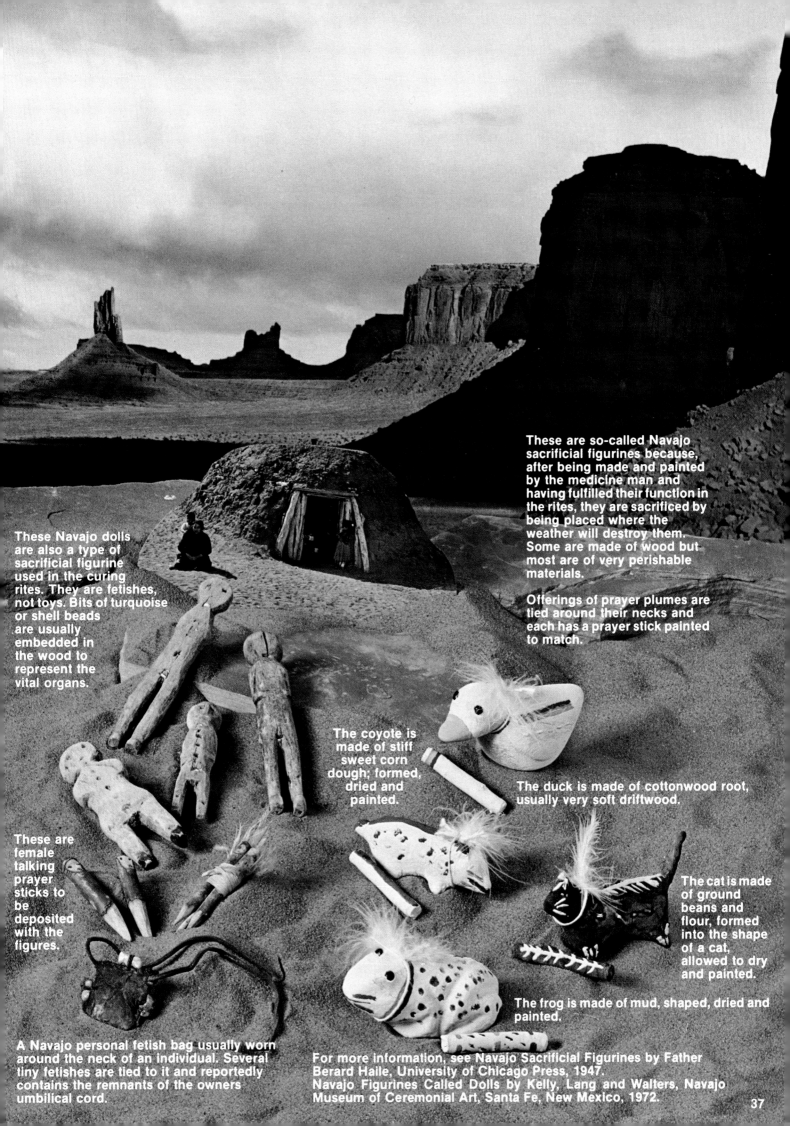

These are so-called Navajo sacrificial figurines because, after being made and painted by the medicine man and having fulfilled their function in the rites, they are sacrificed by being placed where the weather will destroy them. Some are made of wood but most are of very perishable materials.

Offerings of prayer plumes are tied around their necks and each has a prayer stick painted to match.

These Navajo dolls are also a type of sacrificial figurine used in the curing rites. They are fetishes, not toys. Bits of turquoise or shell beads are usually embedded in the wood to represent the vital organs.

The coyote is made of stiff sweet corn dough; formed, dried and painted.

The duck is made of cottonwood root, usually very soft driftwood.

These are female talking prayer sticks to be deposited with the figures.

The cat is made of ground beans and flour, formed into the shape of a cat, allowed to dry and painted.

The frog is made of mud, shaped, dried and painted.

A Navajo personal fetish bag usually worn around the neck of an individual. Several tiny fetishes are tied to it and reportedly contains the remnants of the owners umbilical cord.

For more information, see Navajo Sacrificial Figurines by Father Berard Haile, University of Chicago Press, 1947.
Navajo Figurines Called Dolls by Kelly, Lang and Walters, Navajo Museum of Ceremonial Art, Santa Fe, New Mexico, 1972.

TURQUOISE FETISH NECKLACES

The tabs marked "David" signify the figures on these two necklaces were carved by David Tsikewa. The fine turquoise beads were made by Santo Domingo Indians in New Mexico.

The necklace on the left was made by Leekya Deyuse.

This fine strand fetish necklace made of various kinds of shell, serpentine, jet and turquoise was made at Zuni, New Mexico by the late Delana family. The large bird is made of pink shell.

Turquoise frog mounted in a silver pendant.

Turquoise bear

This necklace by Leekya is made more attractive by having a variety of figures of shell and jet mixed in with the turquoise. It is strung on Domingo Heshe and hanging at the bottom are a pair of turquoise Jaclah or Navajo earrings.

38   Turquoise frog by Neil Natewa

BEARS ON A WOODEN STUMP

Made by
various carvers

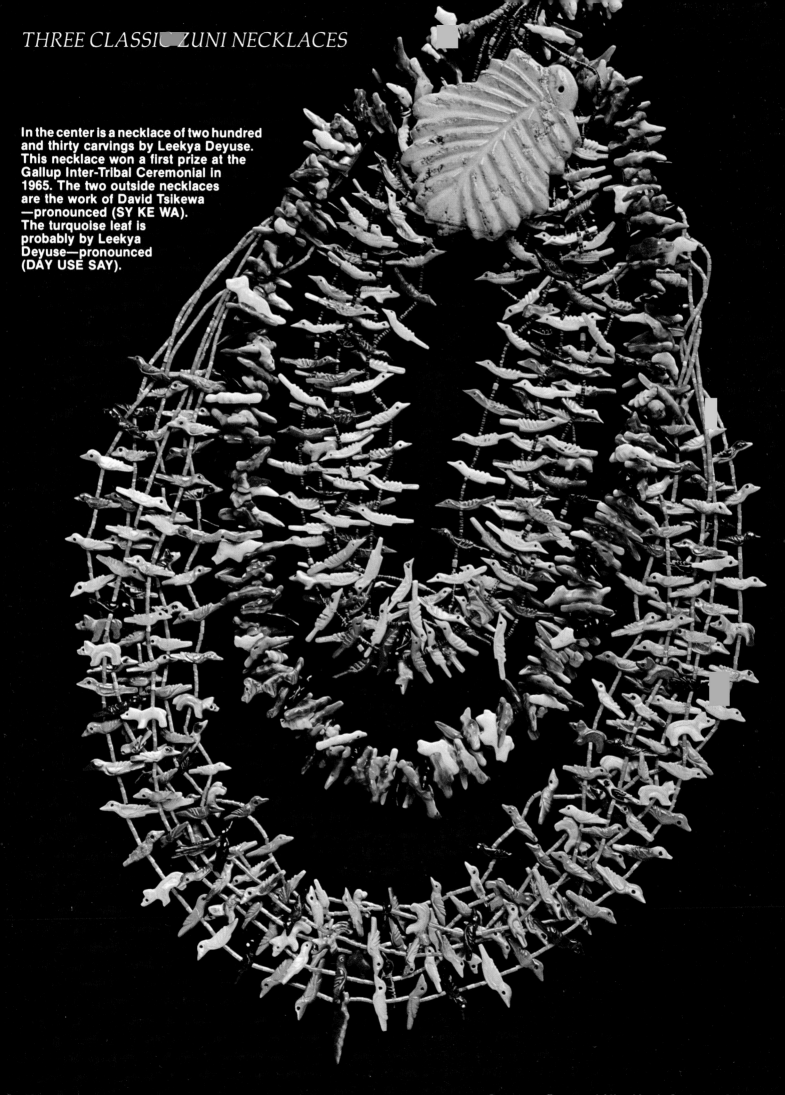

In the center is a necklace of two hundred and thirty carvings by Leekya Deyuse. This necklace won a first prize at the Gallup Inter-Tribal Ceremonial in 1965. The two outside necklaces are the work of David Tsikewa —pronounced (SY KE WA). The turquoise leaf is probably by Leekya Deyuse—pronounced (DAY USE SAY).

Courtesy Don and Nita Hoel, Sedona, Arizona

A pack of black jet foxes with turquoise eyes carved by Tony Luala and strung on coral.

Courtesy Bear Toes Indian Jewelry Gallup, New Mexico

A bear carved from a piece of black mother of pearl shell, inlaid with a coral heart line.

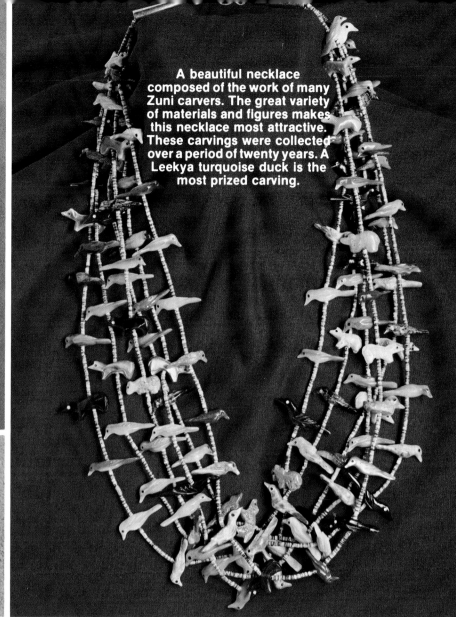

A beautiful necklace composed of the work of many Zuni carvers. The great variety of materials and figures makes this necklace most attractive. These carvings were collected over a period of twenty years. A Leekya turquoise duck is the most prized carving.

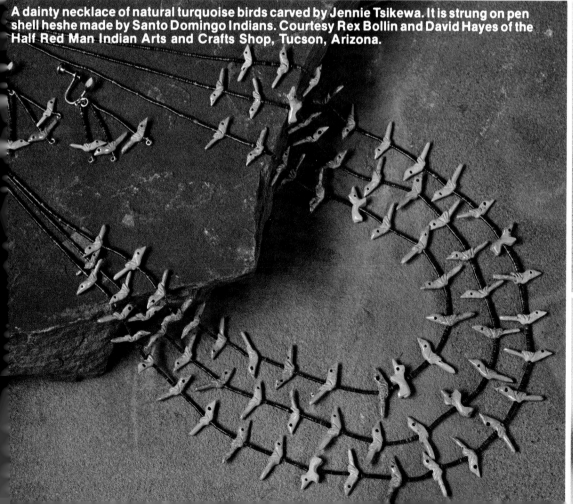

A dainty necklace of natural turquoise birds carved by Jennie Tsikewa. It is strung on pen shell heshe made by Santo Domingo Indians. Courtesy Rex Bollin and David Hayes of the Half Red Man Indian Arts and Crafts Shop, Tucson, Arizona.

A green leaf of turquoise from the Blue Diamond Mine.

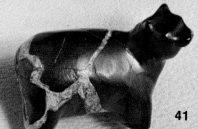

A bear carved from a hematite concretion with calcite veining.

SNAKES

These snake carvings for the most part are not true fetishes but novelty items using the artist's imagination. They are carved from the parts of shells that lend themselves best to the shape of snakes. Slicing the end off of cone shells to make a coiled snake or slicing thru the center of a cameo or helmet shell to make a crawling snake.

This guy is really poisonous.

Courtesy Don and Nita Hoel, Sedona, Arizona

Frog carved of a piece of black lip mother of pearl shell, inlayed with turquoise eyes and spots.

A frog of red abalone shell carved by Leekya Deyuse especially for mounting in jewelry.

Three large turquoise carvings of snakes by Leekya Deyuse made into rings. They are pictured at twice natural size.

Frog of carved amber by Neil Natewa of Zuni.

43

BIG HORN RAMS

Turquoise mole

Two turquoise bison

Two necklaces of coral cardinals by David Tsikewa (Sy Ke Wa).

A typical Leekya necklace, jet birds, carved nuggets and turquoise leaf.

Only the carvings in these bola ties were done by Leekya. A silversmith designed and assembled them.

A pink conch shell frog made for mounting in silver, one of Leekya's specialties.

A turquoise frog carved so it can be mounted in a ring or bracelet.

45

The birds on this lovely necklace were carved from the bright rose pink hinge part of the codakia shell. The beads were made from the flat part of the same shell.

CARVINGS BY LEEKYA DEYUSE

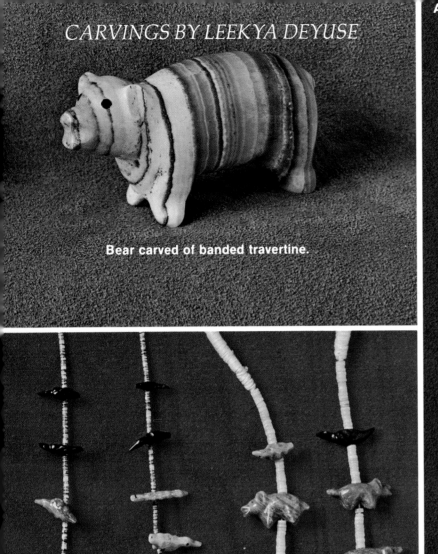

Bear carved of banded travertine.

Two necklaces carved from yellow/green serpentine

Courtesy Don and Nita Hoel
Sedona, Arizona

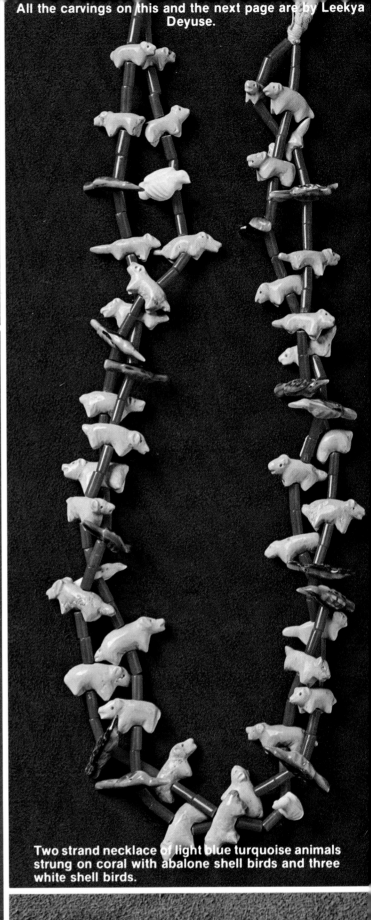

Two strand necklace of light blue turquoise animals strung on coral with abalone shell birds and three white shell birds.

Sheep carved of mottled brown travertine.

A two strand necklace of serpentine, travertine, and turquoise, strung on turquoise beads.

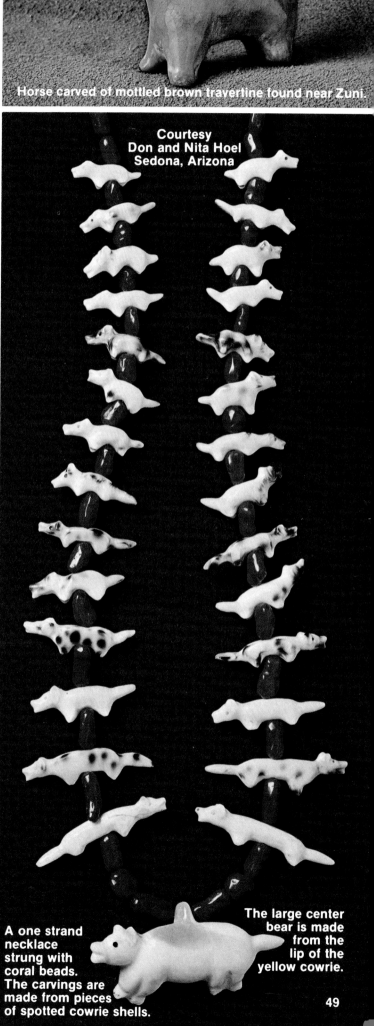

Horse carved of mottled brown travertine found near Zuni.

The large center bear is made from the lip of the yellow cowrie.

A one strand necklace strung with coral beads. The carvings are made from pieces of spotted cowrie shells.

Wolf carved from the lip of pink conch shell

49

Turquoise frog and owl carved by Neil Natewa of Zuni.

SALAMANDERS, LIZARDS AND TURTLES

Red shell

Green serpentine with coral spots

Purple lip oyster

Spotted Cowrie

Catlinite

Turquoise

Jet

Two turquoise frogs carved by David Tsikewa of Zuni.

50

SHELL FROGS

Purple lip rock oyster

These attractive carvings have been made and worn since prehistoric times and are still very popular today.

Red spondylus

White mussel

Glycymeris

Pink mussel

Conch shell

Red spondylus

Red spondylus

Glycymeris

Glycymeris

Glycymeris

Three large frogs of natural turquoise

These and most other frogs are associated with rain and moisture and used in ceremonies about rain-making. Frogs of various materials have been frequently found where they were buried near springs, water holes and near the stream entrance to a lake.

The largest of these frogs weighs two pounds.

FROGS
and Amphibians

Lizard

Turtle

Snake

Turtle

Salamander

Turtle

51

A HANDSOME FETISH NECKLACE

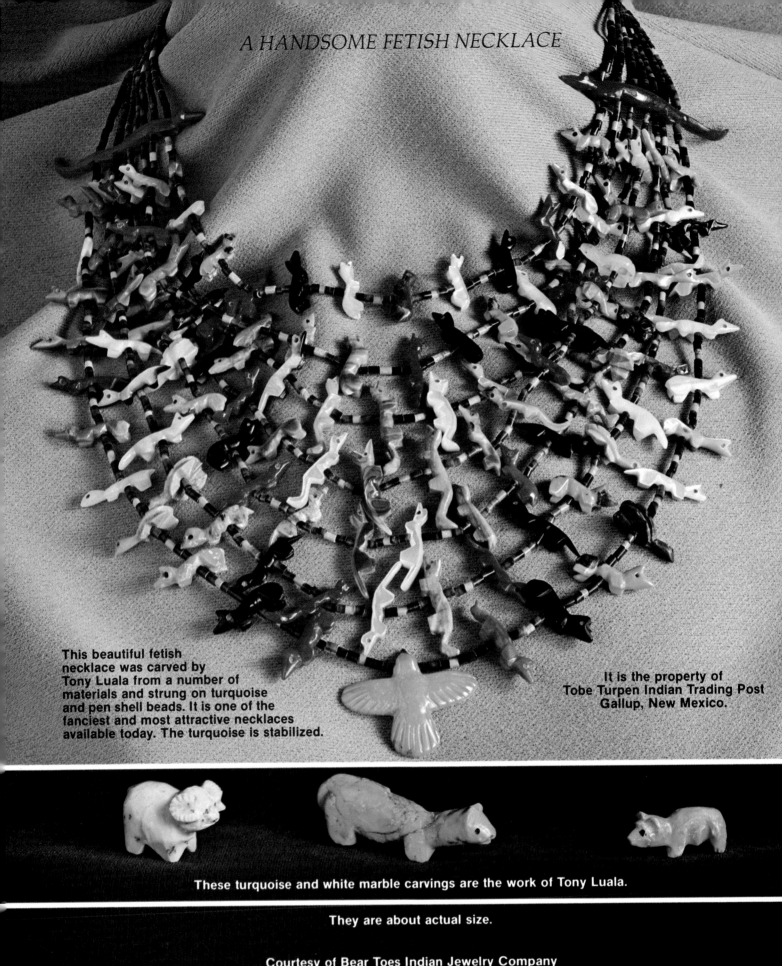

This beautiful fetish necklace was carved by Tony Luala from a number of materials and strung on turquoise and pen shell beads. It is one of the fanciest and most attractive necklaces available today. The turquoise is stabilized.

It is the property of Tobe Turpen Indian Trading Post Gallup, New Mexico.

These turquoise and white marble carvings are the work of Tony Luala.

They are about actual size.

Courtesy of Bear Toes Indian Jewelry Company Gallup, New Mexico

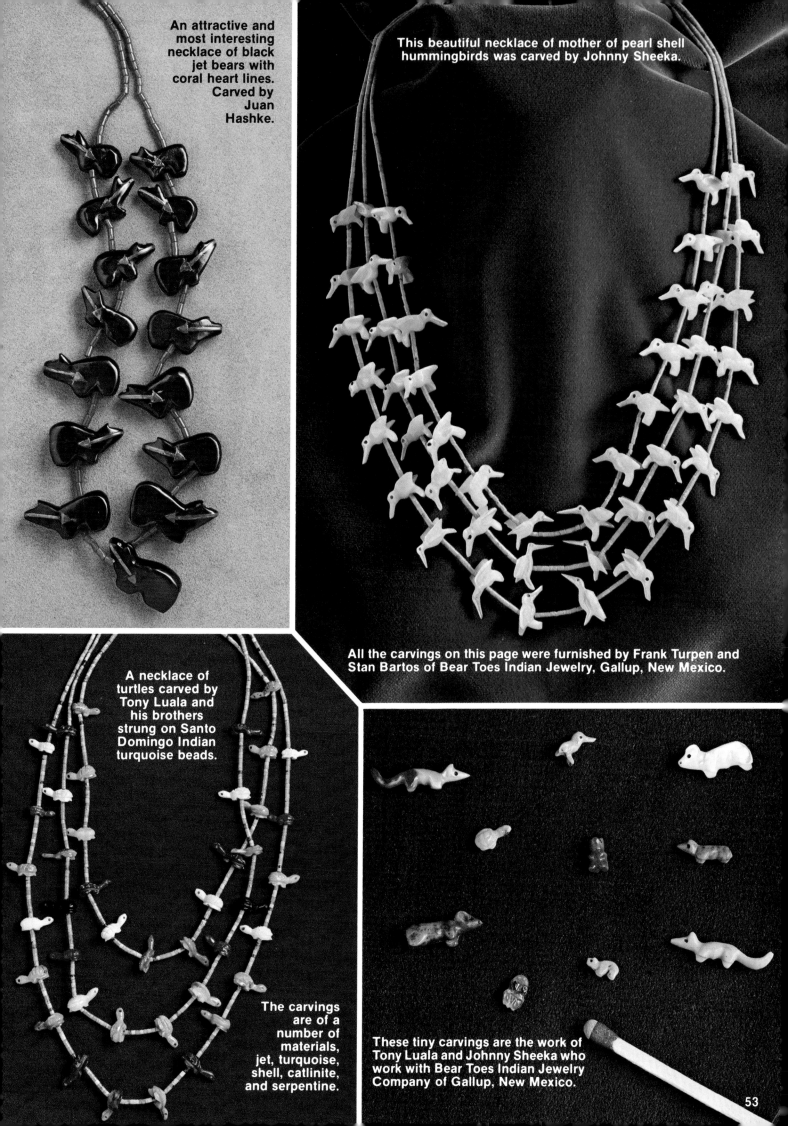

An attractive and most interesting necklace of black jet bears with coral heart lines. Carved by Juan Hashke.

This beautiful necklace of mother of pearl shell hummingbirds was carved by Johnny Sheeka.

A necklace of turtles carved by Tony Luala and his brothers strung on Santo Domingo Indian turquoise beads.

All the carvings on this page were furnished by Frank Turpen and Stan Bartos of Bear Toes Indian Jewelry, Gallup, New Mexico.

The carvings are of a number of materials, jet, turquoise, shell, catlinite, and serpentine.

These tiny carvings are the work of Tony Luala and Johnny Sheeka who work with Bear Toes Indian Jewelry Company of Gallup, New Mexico.

HORSES

DOMESTIC ANIMALS

Wolf
There is a wolf in the herd.

BEARS

These bears are going over the mountain.

Old fetishes of the early 1900's.

Wolf

Bear

Horse

MOUNTAIN LIONS

Probably
a wolf.

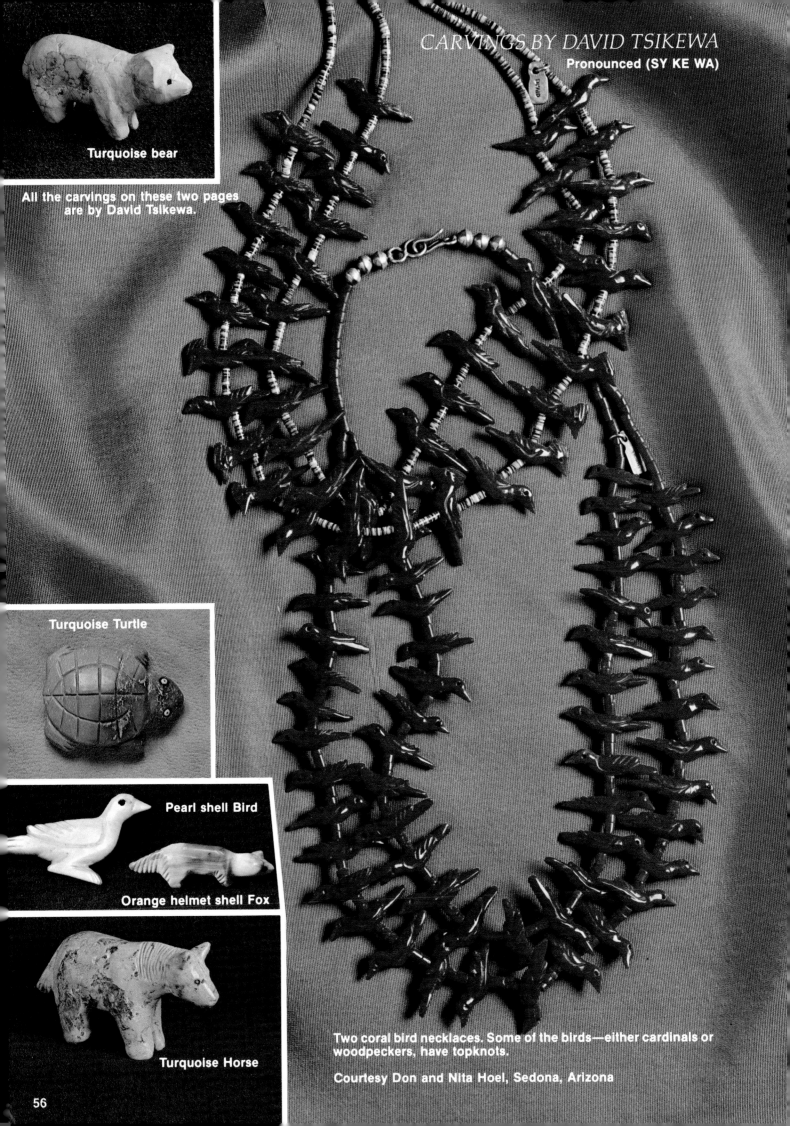

Turquoise bear

All the carvings on these two pages are by David Tsikewa.

CARVINGS BY DAVID TSIKEWA
Pronounced (SY KE WA)

Turquoise Turtle

Pearl shell Bird

Orange helmet shell Fox

Turquoise Horse

Two coral bird necklaces. Some of the birds—either cardinals or woodpeckers, have topknots.

Courtesy Don and Nita Hoel, Sedona, Arizona

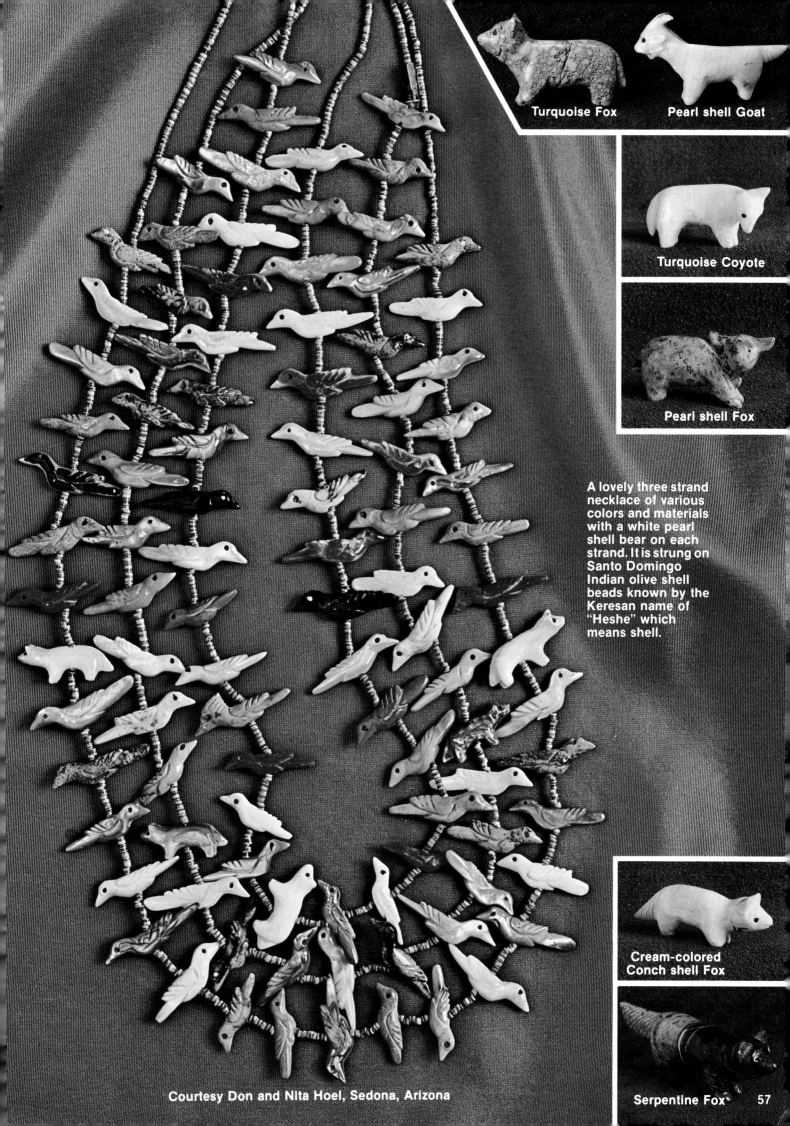

Turquoise Fox

Pearl shell Goat

Turquoise Coyote

Pearl shell Fox

A lovely three strand necklace of various colors and materials with a white pearl shell bear on each strand. It is strung on Santo Domingo Indian olive shell beads known by the Keresan name of "Heshe" which means shell.

Cream-colored Conch shell Fox

Serpentine Fox

Courtesy Don and Nita Hoel, Sedona, Arizona

57

ZUNI TURQUOISE SCULPTURE

Leekya Deyuse

Leo Pablano

Teddy Weahkee

Leekya Deyuse

Leekya Deyuse

Leekya Deyuse

The height in the art of Zuni carving was reached when several traders at Zuni made use of their larger pieces of turquoise by encouraging the best Zuni artists to carve figures in the human form. They produced some of the most intriguingly beautiful statuettes seen anywhere in the world. Their size varies from one inch to about six inches. The usual size is about three to four inches tall. The carvers' names are near each figure.

By using their friends and neighbors as models these artists have given us a rare picture of some of the characters at Zuni.

Leekya Deyuse

Teddy Weahkee

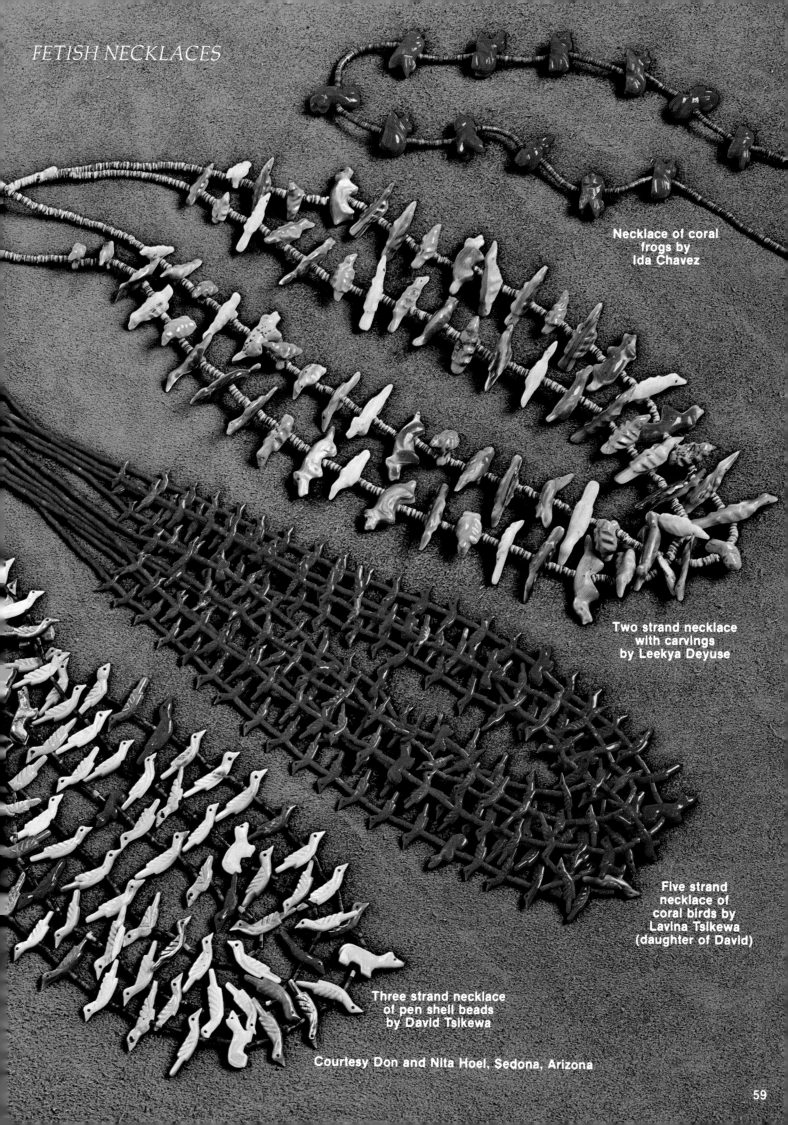

Necklace of coral
frogs by
Ida Chavez

Two strand necklace
with carvings
by Leekya Deyuse

Five strand
necklace of
coral birds by
Lavina Tsikewa
(daughter of David)

Three strand necklace
of pen shell beads
by David Tsikewa

Courtesy Don and Nita Hoel, Sedona, Arizona

A CLASSIC FETISH NECKLACE

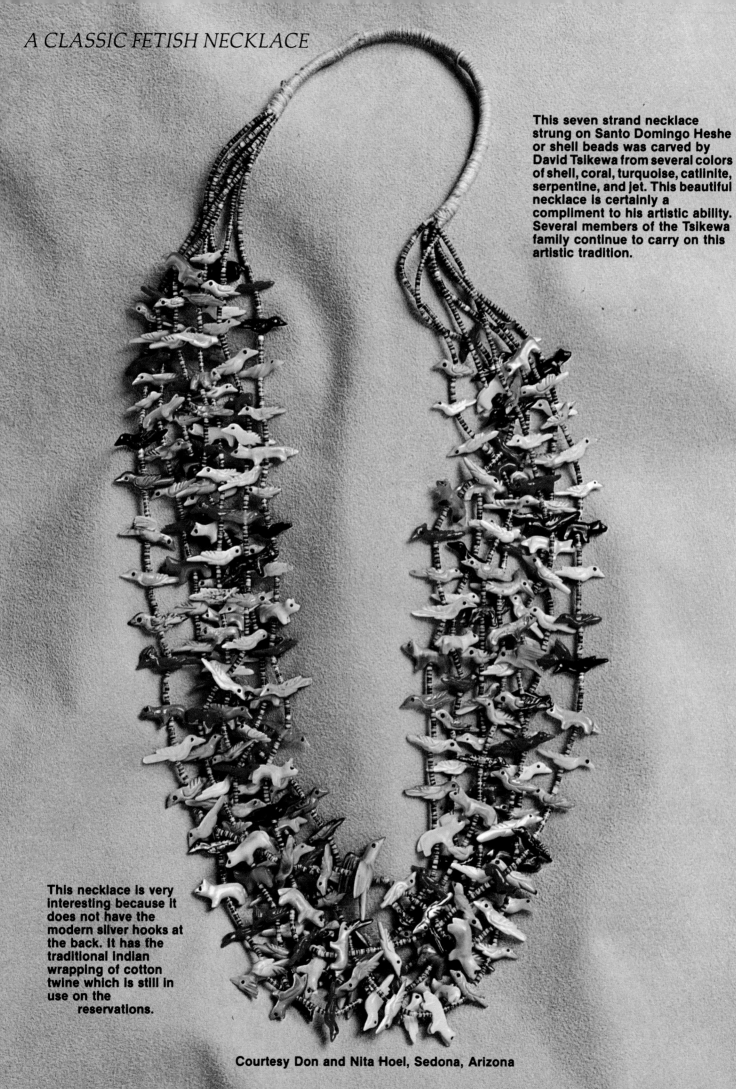

This seven strand necklace strung on Santo Domingo Heshe or shell beads was carved by David Tsikewa from several colors of shell, coral, turquoise, catlinite, serpentine, and jet. This beautiful necklace is certainly a compliment to his artistic ability. Several members of the Tsikewa family continue to carry on this artistic tradition.

This necklace is very interesting because it does not have the modern silver hooks at the back. It has the traditional Indian wrapping of cotton twine which is still in use on the reservations.

Courtesy Don and Nita Hoel, Sedona, Arizona

An enlargement of the center section of the necklace pictured on the preceeding page to show details of carving.

FOREIGN MADE FETISHES

The carvings in these two groups were copied in Italy from fetishes taken over there by importers.

The illustrations on this page are just an attempt to show that there are copies of carvings being made in foreign countries. There are also many copies being made by non-Indians. There are also many fetishes being carved by Indians from tribes whose members never carved a fetish and even had strict taboos against carving them. It is therefore very difficult for the uninformed to tell the difference. The only solution is to buy from a reliable dealer and have him guarantee to refund your money if you are not satisfied that your fetish necklace is authentic.

These carvings are also foreign made—probably in Italy. Others are made in Formosa, Hong Kong, and the Philippine Islands. These are crude and square cut, but there are many done very beautifully and resemble Indian fetishes very closely.

THE SILVER FETISH FIGURE

A very recent innovation or addition to the fetish necklace scene is the small animal and bird fetish cast in silver. It is possible a few were made by hand in the early 1930's when there was a surge of popularity in Indian jewelry. The ones most seen at present are mass produced by the lost wax methods in factories in and around Albuquerque, New Mexico by non-Indians and should not be considered as true fetishes but merely as costume jewelry.

FOREIGN MADE FETISH NECKLACE

All the fetishes in this necklace were carved in Italy and the shell beads or heshe was made in the Philippine Islands.

There are many necklaces of foreign manufacture being sold as genuine Indian-made. The only protection an uninformed person has against this dishonest practice is to buy from reliable dealers

A NOTE TO THE READER

In this book we have attempted to present the reader with a pictorial account of the art of the Southwestern Indian Carver since prehistoric times. It becomes apparent that the carver of a thousand years ago was equally as talented as his modern brother. Due to the fact that he was carving only with primitive tools, his skill seems very ingenious. Although the contemporary fetish necklace appears to be a very modern creation, archeological discoveries have produced many tiny carvings that tend to convince one that the fetish necklace was a popular item over a thousand years ago. The fetish necklace of today is purely an article of adornment and not a good luck charm.

It seems that at certain times or periods down thru the centuries, the wearing of tiny effigies of birds and animals has been very popular. Evidently it is our good fortune to be living during one of these periods of time. By picturing some of the articles used in the fetish ceremonies, we can give only a brief glimpse of the intricate and mysterious beliefs surrounding the making and use of fetishes. It is not the purpose of this book to pry into the secret fetish beliefs but only to try and present a picture to people who otherwise would never become familiar with these beautiful and intriguing creations of the mind of man.

ACKNOWLEDGEMENTS

Like our turquoise book, this book can never be considered a one-man accomplishment. On every hand we have been given the most friendly and generous help and cooperation. I would like to thank the many Indian people and medicine men, Indian traders, archaeologists, anthropologists and the many people of several museums who have given us their most invaluable help and encouragement while we were working on this book. Especially their trust in loaning us their private and cherished possessions while they were being photographed.

I would like to thank two of the best photographers in the world today, Naurice Koonce and Peter Bloomer, for their wonderful cooperation. Their unlimited originality and artistic abilities have made this book possible. Their photographs appear on the following page numbers under their names:

Naurice Koonce
Cover, 3, 4, 5, 6, 7, 8, 9, 11, 12, 13, 14, 15, 16, 17, 20, 21, 22, 23, 24, 25, 26, 27, 28, 29, 30.

Peter Bloomer
5, 10, 12, 16, 18, 19, 24, 28, 30, 31, 32, 33, 34, 35, 38, 39, 40, 42, 44, 45, 47, 49, 51, 54, 55, 56, 57, 59, 60, 61, Back Cover.

I would like to give special thanks to:

Dr. Charles C. DiPeso and Miss Gloria Fenner of The Amerind Foundation, Dragoon, Arizona, for letting us photograph valuable articles in the collections;

Artist Rod Goebel of Taos, New Mexico, for his wonderful cooperation and help in preparing the paintings photographed in this book;

Mrs. Ruth E. Kirk of Santa Fe, New Mexico, and Mr. Tom E. Kirk of La Jolla, California, for the use of the valuable Kirk manuscripts;

Helene Warren of Albuquerque, New Mexico, for advice and loan of valuable material;

Mrs. Maisy Nouck of Phoenix, Arizona

Mr. Jim Tradup who has given me valuable advice from his great store of knowledge in color printing and publication.

Forrest Fenn, Fenn Galleries, Santa Fe, New Mexico

I would like to show special appreciation to Don and Nita Hoel of Sedona, Arizona, for allowing us to invade the privacy of their home and to photograph many of their most cherished possessions. They are most gracious hosts.

Many thanks also to many other people who have given help, advice or direction, and are not mentioned elsewhere in the book:

Mark Bahti	Stanley S. Mahan
Peggy Bahti	Richard Millar
Richard Barret II	Don and Angie Owen
Rex Bollin	Eveli Sabatie
Eddie Gilmore	Frank Thompson
Cecil L. Gutherie	Tobe Turpen
Daved Hayes	Dr. and Mrs. Hershel Thornburg
Dianne E. Mahan	

My thanks to many other people who have given help, advice or direction, and to anyone who has been unintentionally omitted.